Crescendo Publishing Presents

Instant Insights on...

BUSINESS

A Time Management System *for* Creative Entrepreneurs

Minette Riordan, Ph.D.

small guides, BIG IMPACT.

Instant Insights On...

A Time Management System for Creative Entrepreneurs

By Minette Riordan, PhD

ISBN: 978-1-944177-27-0 (p)
ISBN: 978-1-944177-28-7 (e)

Crescendo Publishing, LLC
300 Carlsbad Village Drive
Ste. 108A, #443
Carlsbad, California 92008-2999

www.CrescendoPublishing.com
GetPublished@CrescendoPublishing.com

What You'll Learn in this Book

Following a recent discussion with one of my clients on time management, she asked me, "Minette, how do you do it? We creative entrepreneurs are mad!" I'd just spent an hour coaching her on how to stop feeling overwhelmed and get things done, without feeling like she was sacrificing her creativity.

As a coach who works exclusively with creative entrepreneurs, I laughed. This client was right. I could hear the lyrics from the famous song "Don't Fence Me In" playing in my head. Creative entrepreneurs resist planning, dislike systems, and are notorious procrastinators. How do I know? Because I am one! But I am also a successful entrepreneur who now knows that without some creative time-management skills, I will never be able to reach my financial goals or build the business that will support the creative lifestyle I want.

In this book, you will discover the time management system that I designed just for creative entrepreneurs. I guarantee the strategies will be fun, colorful, and playful, and they will get you on the path to productivity. No more late nights feeling overwhelmed and exhausted. No more working weekends instead of spending time with your loved ones. Once you implement even just one or two of these strategies, you will see a significant improvement in your mood, your use of time, and your creative output!

In this book, you'll get *Instant Insights* on...

- Why time management is a challenge for creative entrepreneurs
- The intimate connection between time and money
- How to make friends with time
- The myths of multitasking and balance
- Why commitment is the first step to making friends with time
- How to carve out more time for yourself and your family
- What systems work best for creative entrepreneurs

A Gift from the Author

To support you in implementing the strategies mentioned in this book and to get the most value out of the content, I have prepared some bonus materials I know you'll love! I created a video series demonstrating several of the strategies, along with a printable handbook with checklists and forms mentioned in the book.

You can access these at
www.pathtoprofitacademy.com/time-management-book

Table of Contents

Successful People Know How to Manage Time......................3

Time Management Starts with Your Big Why........................9

Time Management is Like Juggling 15

A Time-Management Checklist...19

Tackle Your Time-Eating Gremlins..25

Conduct a Time Audit..31

Time to Clear the Cobwebs...39

Why To-Do Lists and Sticky Notes Don't Work 45

Next Step: Add Your Big Six to Your Calendar 55

Make Your Planning Visual – Mind Maps................................61

Time Blocking Will Become Your Best Friend.......................65

Change Your Business or Go Out of Business:
How Committed Are You? 71

About the Author 77

Connect with the Author..83

Other Books by this Author 85

In Dedication

This book is dedicated to all of my amazing clients who have used these systems and given me feedback on what works and what doesn't for creative, visual thinkers and dreamers. I am so proud of each of you and all the beautiful ways you are changing the world!

It's also dedicated to my wonderful husband, Brad, for his patience and love. It's not easy living with a creative entrepreneur!

Successful People Know How to Manage Time

People ask me all the time, "How do you get so much done? You always seem to be so busy!" I shrug and smile. My life is wonderfully full these days. I know what it takes to build a profitable business, and I am willing to put in the time to create the lifestyle and the financial freedom I want for myself and my family. I heard a speaker once talk about the cult of "Busy" and how it seems to be a badge of honor that women wear to prove our worth. However, there is a difference between being busy for the sake of being busy and being productive. As you read through this book, I invite you to look at your relationship with time.

My secret to time management is to be intentional with how I spend my time, during working hours and leisure time. When I am not intentional with my time, I find myself feeling overwhelmed, resentful, and stressed out. I have been an entrepreneur for over fifteen years. I am also a wife, and my husband and I recently celebrated our twentieth wedding anniversary. I am a mom to two fabulous teens whose lives are just as busy as mine. I love to volunteer in my community and attend my kids' activities. I also like to write and to make art. I love beach walks at low tide and enjoying a glass of wine at a local winery. It's a lot and I don't get it right all the time, but when I get stuck, I go back to the systems I teach you in this book to help me get into action again.

Time management is the key to financial success.

In order to manage our time effectively, we need to have clear goals and a clear path to get us there. We also have to have strong boundaries. We have to learn to say "no" powerfully to invitations or requests that take us off the path, which isn't simple or easy, but it is necessary.

There are only twenty-four hours in a day. We cannot change that. However, we can use the time we have more effectively. I was at an event a couple years ago when I had this huge aha moment. In that moment I realized I was not taking myself or my business seriously; I was treating it like a hobby. I was not doing what needed to be done to make money in my business. I was afraid to invest time, money, and energy into building my business, knowing that this would take me away from my beloved family. I needed to shift my mindset.

When I came home and shared this realization with my husband, he laughed. But he also said that he would do whatever it would take to support me in creating a profitable business and that I shouldn't worry about traveling and being away. We were clear that our goal was to get him out of his job as soon as possible. It would take some effort and some sacrifice in order for me to be able to create enough income to make that happen. Once I shifted my mindset and prioritized my time, the money and clients began to flow in.

It's now two years later, and my husband has quit his full-time job to come support me in growing our coaching and training business. This has been a dream of ours for a while, yet it was a scary decision to make. We had to up our game in a big way. I am now the primary moneymaker, and how I spend my time has to reflect that shift. It's meant missing a few of the kids' concerts and activities, being out of town on my husband's birthday, and being gone almost as much as I am home.

It's not always easy or fun for any of us. But the payoffs are there, too. I love working with my husband and having him beside me as a sounding board and another body to share the work of building a business and raising a family. He was present before, but the shared commitment is empowering in a whole new way.

And I love how we are able to continue to be present for our kids. One of us is always home when they get home from school. They come and sit and talk to us about their day. Yes, they complain about how much I travel and work, but they also know how important it is to sustaining our way of life. We try to engage and involve them as much as possible. I often take our fourteen-year-old daughter to networking events with me, and both kids will help out at our live events this year. We are actively working to model what it looks like to lead a very full life as a successful entrepreneur.

Successful people know how to manage time. I have heard my mentors talk about how tightly they manage their calendar. There's no success without it. Do you feel that you're as busy as you can be, but you are not achieving even a fraction of what you say you want? This book will show you how to use your innate creativity to create simple systems and structures so that you can start working smarter, not harder.

Your Instant Insights...

- Stop being busy and start being productive.
- Time management is the secret to financial success.
- Start treating your business like a business, not a hobby.

Time Management Starts with Your Big Why

I am heartbroken to find so many women struggling with guilt, worry, stress, and anxiety. They feel torn between family and business, but it shouldn't have to be that way!

We became entrepreneurs because we are passionate about the work we do and we want the opportunity to serve more people. But we want to do it without sacrificing the quality time our kids and husbands deserve. I know that it takes courage to make hard choices, to make sacrifices, and sometimes to work long hours.

I owned a publishing company for eleven years. We printed a monthly parenting magazine and hosted huge expos twice a year. I can remember too many days, nights, and weekends when I was struggling to get everything done to get an issue of my parenting magazine to the printer. I was exhausted and short-tempered, and I couldn't afford to pay for others to help me—or at least I believed I couldn't. My family definitely wasn't getting the best of me.

I remember feeling so tired that I could barely stand up and my kids saying, "Please, Mommy, will you play with me?"

Surely this wasn't why I started my business. Not only was I working too hard, I wasn't paying myself. My company was grossing hundreds of thousands of dollars, but at the end of the month, I always seemed to be asking, "Where's my money?" I learned a lot of difficult lessons during those eleven years, but the most important lesson I learned was that systems liberate you.

I didn't want to believe it. I loved going with the flow. I am a hard worker and have a huge capacity for getting things done. But often I wasn't doing the right things. I was resisting or putting off the tasks that would enable me to make more money, such as making more sales calls or collecting on overdue payments. Inevitably these were the tasks that took courage to get going.

I remember so clearly sitting down with my accountant at tax time one year. She looked at me and said, "Minette, you should have paid yourself $77,000 this year." I looked at her in shock. "Where's my money?" I asked. This was a huge turning point for me in that business and ultimately led to us making the difficult decision to sell the publishing company and move to California.

It was time to dig deep and get crystal clear about what I really wanted. I discovered that courage stemmed from understanding my motivation to build a profitable business. Being a creative entrepreneur is not for the faint of heart and I can't imagine being anything else.

In fact, I invite you to ask yourself right now, "Why do I want to make money? Why do I want to be of service to others?" At the end of the day, to enjoy the entrepreneurial lifestyle, you have to make some hard decisions, refocus on your core values, and get insanely clear about your BIG WHY. Your BIG WHY is what reminds you every day to get up, to keep going, and to take risks. Knowing your BIG WHY will help you stand in the place of courage on a daily basis, even when life seems impossible.

My BIG WHY is FREEDOM! Freedom for myself, my family, and my clients. Freedom to live life on my terms. It also means time freedom and financial freedom. Freedom is at the core of everything that I do and why I do it.

Knowing your BIG WHY will also help you make better decisions about how you choose to spend your time because the truth is, you have complete control of your time if you are an entrepreneur. You have the freedom to decide in each and every moment how you want spend your time. Yes, I know—you have commitments, kids, spouses, deadlines ... but let's be honest. Why are you in business?

Life will always test us, interrupt us, and provide a kaleidoscope of distractions. Rather than always focusing on the million small tasks that need to get done, I encourage you to practice making more intentional decisions on a day-to-day basis that move you forward on all fronts. Start by repeatedly asking yourself:

- Is this in alignment with what I want the most?
- Is this the best next step I need to take right now?

I tell my clients, "When intuition tells you it's time to get off the phone and go talk to your kids, trust and do it. When intuition tells you to make one more sales call, do it."

Learning to trust your intuition is a process; the more you practice listening to and trusting yourself, the more successful you will be.

Moving through fear toward courage is all about making decisions—big ones and little ones! If you find that you are stuck in fear and indecision and feeling overwhelmed, I invite you to download my free core values assessment. Reconnecting to your core values is a great place to start discovering your BIG WHY; to get back in alignment with yourself, your business, and your family; and to learn to make decisions based on your values, not your feelings of fear or guilt. You can download a free version of this assessment here: www. pathtoprofitacademy.com/time-management-book.

A sense of calm and clarity come from knowing exactly who you are and what you want to create. Stop chasing the dream everyone else says you should want, and start focusing on YOUR DREAM!

It is absolutely possible to build a profitable business in thirty hours a week or less when you focus on the right actions to take every day. This book is all about working smarter, not harder.

You had the courage to start your business. Now have the courage to turn it into the vision of success that you want. Go! Start now!

Your Instant Insights...

- Get crystal clear about your BIG WHY. Knowing what you value most will help you make better decisions about how to use your time.

- Trust your intuition when it tells you to take time off or to make one more sales call.

- Systems liberate you.

Time Management is Like Juggling

I don't believe that work-life balance is possible. I think it's a myth that there is some perfect world where everything in our life gets equal amounts of attention. That's an unrealistic perspective. And I think the media is doing women everywhere a disservice by barraging us with some mistaken belief that this is what we are supposed to be striving for. Rather than trying to achieve some ideal lifestyle where you get to do it all, have it all, and be it all (whatever "all" means), I invite you to make time for what matters most.

The life of the creative entrepreneur is more like a juggling act than a balancing act. Because we love to do so many different things, we often juggle many different roles. And although we love all of them, we find our attention being pulled in too many directions. When we do drop one of the balls, blame and self-judgment often stop us from moving forward. We allow our self-care to fall to the bottom of the to-do list and often feel too tired to enjoy time with our kids and spouses.

In this scenario, guilt can be crippling, especially for those of us with loved ones clamoring for our attention. When this happens, go back to your core values and your BIG WHY to determine where you are out of alignment. Course correct, shift directions, or take a whole day off to do nothing. Your time is your own. Begin to see time as your friend instead of your enemy.

Most of the time I love juggling the many different areas of my life, but I notice that when I'm distracted or divided, I start to drop too many balls. Sometimes I drop all the balls and collapse in front of the television with a glass of wine and the cat on my lap. Usually some downtime and a good night's sleep are enough to get me back on track.

When you start to notice that you are dropping too many balls and spending too much time on the couch, take a five- or ten-minute time-out. Sit quietly and take several deep breaths. Allow yourself to be present in the moment.

Take out your journal and write down three to five things that you feel grateful for right now. After you write them down, read them aloud (or silently) to yourself and say thank you. Then ask yourself, "What is one step I can take right now to get back on track?" Write it down and then go do it. Trust your intuition, even if you hear something like, "Take a walk," "Doodle," or "Dig in the garden."

Your Instant Insights...

- Do what's most important first.
- Your life is a juggling act, and sometimes it's okay to drop all the balls and take a break.
- Dropping too many balls? Take a time-out to express gratitude for what is working.

A Time-Management Checklist

As we continue to focus on what types of time-management strategies and systems work best for creative entrepreneurs, we need to do a quick assessment of how you are spending your time.

Below, you will find a series of statements about the current state of your business and your life. Answer the statements with "always," "sometimes," or "never." Take a moment to acknowledge and celebrate the good habits you already have in place. This list is not intended to be comprehensive. It's intended to be a snapshot of the most important balls that you need to keep juggling.

As you go through the list, notice how you feel about each statement. If a negative thought comes to the surface, acknowledge it and let it go. It's just a thought, not a reality. Nothing on this list is impossible to establish in your life. Pay special attention to the statements that you resist. Again, just notice them and ask yourself, "Why am I feeling so much resistance?"

- I regularly set goals, plan, and prioritize on a daily, weekly, monthly, and long-term basis.

- I have consistent structures and systems in place to support me.

- I practice good time-management skills and am diligent with my calendar.

- I regularly take time off for holidays and long weekends.

- I have a clear line between home and work, even if I work at home.

- I spend regular, quality time with loved ones.

- I make time for friends.

- I ask for help when I need it.

- I am good at saying "no" to projects or people that take too much time and energy.

- I am okay with "good enough" versus "perfect."

- I get regular exercise.

- I eat healthy foods.

- I enjoy a regular spiritual practice.

- I reward myself for my success!

- I am positive, passionate, and enthusiastic—every day!

Reflecting back on your responses, notice any trends. Are you doing a great job of taking care of yourself at home but avoiding work? Are you so focused on work you have forgotten you have a personal life?

Now that you have completed this quick assessment, let's take it to another level. Take out your journal or some blank sheets of paper. Grab some markers or your favorite pen and let's dig a little deeper into your experience of time. You can download a copy of this assessment above and this journaling activity here: www. pathtoprofitacademy.com/time-management-book.

Connecting to your Truth through Journaling

What is your **TRUTH** about struggling with some of these areas of time management? Pick three areas from the checklist that you would like to improve, and answer the following three questions for each statement.

- What is the **IMPACT** of not mastering this; how it is affecting your life and/or your business?

- What is the most powerful **DECISION** you need to make to improve this?

- What is one **ACTION** you will take, and by when will you take it?

Here is an example:

I chose the phrase "I eat healthy foods."

This is an area of my life that needs improvement and yet the truth is I don't always make time for improvement.

The impact of not mastering this is that I don't feel great, I don't have as much energy for all the things I want and need to do and I don't love the way I look.

The most powerful decision I can make to improve this is to commit to eating healthfully and to make it a priority.

One action I can take is to create a meal plan for the week and only shop for what I plan to eat. Another example might be cleaning out the pantry and getting rid of unhealthy snacks that are easy to reach for.

Follow this process for each statement and notice the connections and actions that you could take. Are you committed to taking these actions? If so, add them to the calendar!

Your Instant Insights...

- Do a quick assessment of how you are spending your time.

- Notice what is working and what you would like to change.

- Commit to taking one action this week that will create a better foundation for time management.

Tackle Your Time-Eating Gremlins

Are you constantly saying, "I don't have enough time"? Or maybe, "I'm too busy"? Or even, "I wish someone could help me manage my time"? That seems to be a constant theme with my coaching clients. Their biggest concern is not having enough hours in the day to get everything done. The thought of adding more to their already full schedule completely overwhelms them. But is lack of time really the challenge?

In this chapter, we tackle the time-eating gremlins you are aware of. In the next chapter, I share how to do a time audit so that you can uncover the time wasters you aren't aware of! I want to share with you some ways that you may be wasting time or underestimating how much time you have. We all have these gremlins, those things that take up our precious time, interrupt us, and stop us from being as productive as we say we want to be. We can't figure out why we never have any time. Our calendar doesn't look that full, does it?

Time management may not be the real problem; it's just the symptom. Here are some possible activities that may be eating up your work time—especially if you are an entrepreneur working from home. Add to the mix your kids, spouse, and the dog begging to get walked, and this list grows exponentially.

- Underestimating how much time a project will take
- Overestimating how much time a project will take
- Spending too much time making to-do lists that are too long
- Checking your e-mail constantly
- Jumping onto social media every time you get a notification
- Watching television two or more hours a day
- Letting paperwork and bills pile up
- Doing laundry or other housework instead of making sales calls
- Meeting with people in person instead of by phone or Skype
- Wasting time looking for things (keys, kids' shoes, the overdue bill, or the permission slip for today's field trip)

- Spending too much time on volunteer activities
- Spending too much time socializing during work hours

The list of activities that can distract any entrepreneur is endless. Because creative entrepreneurs tend to avoid or ignore the work they don't want to do, these make great distractions. Over and over again I see creative entrepreneurs failing to make their marketing or other moneymaking activities a priority during prime work hours.

Sometimes fear lies underneath those distractions, in which case we tend to create more activities and make ourselves busy so that we don't have to focus on what is or isn't working in our business. Fear of making sales calls can have us scrubbing floorboards instead of picking up the phone. I was choosing to spend time on activities that were not moving me forward.

These are very real fears, and I have dealt with all of them at various times in my career. I still struggle at times to get all the pieces of family and business flowing in harmony. How do I do it when it's working well? I have my priorities in the right order, and I manage my time effectively.

Here are some strategies I have taught my clients to help them manage their time:

- Use a timer for tasks like social media. Set a timer for fifteen minutes, and just focus on tasks related to your business, like posting an update or responding to engagement on your business pages. It's easy to get caught in the rabbit hole of social media, especially when you work from home.

- Turn off your e-mail notifications and check your email only two or three times per day. It's amazing how much time this saves!

- Break bigger projects down into bite-size steps. Don't expect to complete an entire project at once. This will help manage expectations about how long a project will take.

- Do the hardest tasks first each day. This might be writing a blog post or making sales calls.

Your Instant Insights...

- Become aware of your time-eating activities.
- Reflect on why you are creating these distractions.
- Commit to taking one action that will save you time this week.

Conduct a Time Audit

In the last section, we talked about time wasters you are aware of. Now it's time to discover other time wasters lurking in your calendar. If you feel unproductive, overwhelmed, and like there is not enough time in the day to grow your business, get exercise, and spend time with loved ones, then I encourage you to do a time audit.

I started using this tool with my coaching clients because they kept sharing their concerns about time flying, having to-do lists that were daunting, and feeling overwhelmed by all the tasks necessary to grow their business.

A time audit is simply tracking your time for at least one workweek, from the moment you get up in the morning until you go to bed at night. There are several simple ways to do this.

- Create a chart, either on a sheet of paper or in your journal (which is my preference as I am more likely to keep track of it). You can download a sample of a hand-drawn version here:

  www.pathtoprofitacademy.com/time-management-book.

- Use a Word document or create a spreadsheet in Excel or Google docs to track online.

- Finally, there are a variety of apps for your smart phone that make this simple for those of you who love technology. One excellent app is ATracker. It's easy to use and creates beautiful, colorful graphs and charts so that you can see how you are spending your time.

What all of these methods have in common is that they are visual. You cannot keep all of this information in your head! You need to capture it in a way that is simple and fun for you.

Some experts recommend tracking your time in fifteen-minute increments. This would drive me crazy, but it would be very thorough. When I audited my time, I used thirty-minute increments.

You should also track tasks and pay attention to how much time they take. Some tasks seem overwhelming to start, but they don't take as long as you think once you actually sit down to do them.

Here's what my client Kristina said she realized from tracking her time: "I'm learning that I'm spending more time on my business than I thought. I can see where I need to spend more time on activities like networking, follow-ups, supporting team members, social networking, etc. I am also learning where I want more balance in my life. I need to spend more time with friends, which fills me up so I have more energy and enthusiasm to give to my business."

Another client, Brittany, realized she was spending too much time checking e-mail and not leaving herself enough long periods of time to do the creative work for her clients. This was causing her tons of stress and frustration. We made a few simple tweaks to her calendar and put a system in place where she checked her e-mail only a few times a day. This is a challenging habit to keep (for me too), but I know that it works.

Are you ready to do your time audit? Under step one below, the blank spaces are included so that you can add any potential time wasters not already covered. When I added up how much time I spend on some of these activities, the results were staggering. Even though I am pretty organized and get a lot done, I discovered I spend more time than I thought on some of these activities, especially checking e-mail and watching TV.

Step One: How many hours per week do you spend:

Checking e-mail:
Watching TV:
Surfing the net:
Napping:
Sleeping:
On the phone:
Arguing:
Instant messaging:
On social media:

_____

_____

_____

_____

_____

_____

Total Hours:

Step Two: What Are You Wasting Most of Your Time Doing?

Simply identify your three worst time wasters from above.

Worst Time Wasters (include # of hours)
1. _____current no. of hours per day:_____
2. _____current no. of hours per day:_____
3. _____current no. of hours per day:_____

Step Three: How Much Time Can You Save?

Now, how much are you willing to cut back on these time wasters and start replacing them with more productive activities? Track the time you spent doing the above activities this week, and see if you can improve with fewer hours in at least three areas.

For example, if you often spend two or three hours a day watching TV, are you willing to cut that back to one hour a day? That one cut could save you ten hours a week.

1. _____ new no. of hours per day:_____
2. _____ new no. of hours per day:_____
3. _____ new no. of hours per day:_____

Step Four: Total # of Hours Saved Per Week:

_____

Once you realize you have been wasting time, it's also crucial to discern what activities should replace the time wasters. Intentional, preplanned activities will help you create the success you seek without overwhelming you or making you feel like you just keep working harder with nothing to show for it.

In the next section, we start looking at strategies for deciding how to spend your time.

Your Instant Insights...

- Conduct a time audit to determine exactly how you are spending your time.

- Discover how much time you are wasting on your time-eating gremlins.

- Commit to cutting back on your top three time wasters.

Time to Clear the Cobwebs

We've talked about a variety of time wasters and how we manage to fill our time with activities that aren't in alignment with our goals. There's one more area that we need to clear when it comes to time management and that is clutter—especially for us creative entrepreneurs who struggle to get stuff done.

I'm not talking about piles of paper on your desk or stacks of business cards you never got around to organizing—although that can be a problem, too. In this case, though, we're talking about the clutter in your head. You know, that endless list of things that continually scrolls through your mind and distracts you just when you're finally ready to focus.

That's the kind of clutter that's really holding you back, and we all have it. The good news is that it's easier to clean up this type of clutter than those piles of paper on the desk, the floor, and the bookshelf—and we're going to do it with an artful, playful brain dump.

I teach all my clients to use this fun, creative process so that they can manage their time better and stop feeling overwhelmed!

Here's how it works:

1. Set aside thirty to sixty minutes of uninterrupted time. It's important that you have a quiet place with no distractions—either internal or external—to derail the process, so plan a time when the kids are at school and you don't have clients calling you. And yes, you can find this time in your calendar. See the chapter on conducting a time audit if you don't believe me.

2. Grab your list-writing tool of choice. This could be a journal, index cards, sticky notes, or blank paper. Make sure you have pencils and/or pens, too. I personally love to use large sheets of inexpensive drawing paper and lots of markers—the more creative and fun the process, the more likely I am to do it.

3. Just write. Make a big list of everything that's on your mind, from getting the dog groomed to building a new website. Whatever you're keeping on that big to-

do list in your head goes into your brain dump. No task is too big or too small, and don't worry about the details yet or all the steps involved in completing a particular task.

4. Once you've got everything out of your head and down on paper, it's time to bring some order to the chaos. Now that you have this massive brain dump of tasks and to-do's all in one place where you can see them, it's time to reorganize your list according to project. Then order your projects by priority, and finally order the tasks within your projects in their logical order. Fill in the blanks where necessary.

   Visit www.pathtoprofitacademy.com/time-management-book for a visual sample of this process.

5. Transfer your brain dump to a trusted calendar system. Your brain dump will do you no good at all if you still feel the need to keep stuff in your head, so this step is critical to your success. Whether your to-do lists are on paper or electronic, you must transfer your newly organized brain dump into a system you trust and use.

I tell my clients to keep a separate journal or notebook just for their brain dumps. I encourage them to do this process daily—before bed or first thing in the morning are good times. It helps you clear the clutter so that you can approach sleep or the next day feeling refreshed and ready to go, not wondering what on earth you should do first.

In the next section I share why brain dumps are better than to-do lists and how to prioritize your tasks so that you are getting everything done.

Whenever you find yourself struggling with feeling overwhelmed or not getting things done, that means it's time to schedule another brain dump. Doing so regularly will help you continue to move forward toward your goals and get the work done.

Your Instant Insights...

- Mental clutter impacts your productivity and creativity.

- Clear your mental cobwebs on a regular basis by allowing yourself time for a brain dump.

- Make the brain dump a regular, creative project that you look forward to.

Why To-Do Lists and Sticky Notes Don't Work

Well, maybe a few sticky notes ... we can't eradicate them completely, can we? In fact, I show you a fun way to use sticky notes in your planning in another section. But right now it's time to tear up your traditional to-do list. You know which one I'm talking about, right? The one that's several pages long and includes a mishmash of business and personal to-do's. "Pay the gas bill" is right below "call the vet" and right above "return a potential client's phone call."

I have many clients who get downright panicky when I tell them that they need to tear up their to-do lists. They don't believe they can function without them. They start freaking out about all those balls they are juggling and wondering how they can possibly survive without a list.

What most of them don't realize is that their exhaustive to-do lists are actually limiting their productivity. I'm not saying that the individual tasks are not important; I'm saying that the traditional to-do list is dysfunctional and doesn't work for creative entrepreneurs.

You may not even use a to-do list, preferring to scribble notes on any scrap of paper at hand, allowing these scraps to float, stack, disappear, reappear, and get lost. You probably find yourself spending way too much time scrambling to find your notes and not enough time actually doing whatever was on the sticky note.

If you are regularly doing your brain dump as described in the last section, then that can serve as your master to-do list. Also remember to look at your business and financial goals to make sure your to-do's are connected to your goals.

When your brain dump is complete, you will need to prioritize your list. I'm going to walk you through a process for how to do this. Once you get the hang of this, it will go quickly, and it won't take as long to do it in the future. You will also understand why not every single task needs to go on your daily to-do list.

Create Your Daily Big Six

One of the reasons that your life feels out of balance and you feel like you never have enough time is that you are not focusing on your priorities.

During this process, we are going to create a list that has no more than six items on it. Yes, I just said "six." This is the secret to productivity, time management, and balance, all rolled into one simple system.

"Big Six" even sounds better than "to-do." Our to-do's are often just busywork that clutters our calendar and our minds. When we focus on what we get to do rather than what we have to do, our mindset shifts into a new gear, and we look forward to the day's work ahead.

If you implement this process daily, I guarantee it will change your life.

Step One

First, go through your brain dump or to-do lists and be brutally honest with yourself about each item. Ask yourself these five questions:

1. Am I ever going to do this (especially that item that shows up week after week, such as finishing a book, a painting, or a home-repair project)? If the answer is "no," take it off your list.

2. Could I ask someone else (kids, spouse, another family member, etc.) to do this?

3. Could I pay someone else to do this?

4. Does this have to be completed by the end of this week?

5. Will this move me closer to or farther away from my goal? (This works for business as well as personal to-do's.)

Step Two

Grab your markers or pen and start crossing off any items that you are not going to do yourself or that will not move you closer to your goals. Put a big colorful star or check mark by the ones you are committed to doing this week. Put another symbol beside the items that can wait until later.

Step Three

Add any new items to the list that might come up because of your new perspective (e.g., hire someone to finish painting the bathroom; hire someone to help with taxes).

Step Four

Look at the list carefully and start to prioritize by day of the week. Take into account both your personal and professional to-do's. Pick the six you commit to doing on Monday before you go to bed! If six feels like too many, pick five or three. It's not the number that matters; it's the commitment to getting them done.

What successful entrepreneurs and CEOs understand is that each day will be full of distractions, interruptions, and unexpected tasks. By putting only a few items on your must-do list each day, you create time and space for the messiness of life. Because creative entrepreneurs are easily distracted by those bright, shiny ideas—the phone call from a friend or the invitation to lunch—it's vital to your business success that you commit to making some progress every single day.

I was serious when I said that time management is the secret to financial success. When we learn to prioritize tasks relevant to making us money, we create a new mindset around how we choose to spend our time.

How Do You Know Which Six to Pick?

Your Big Six can include a combination of personal and professional tasks. Start by looking at your long list and pick the most urgent first. Items that have deadlines attached like "pay a bill" or "call the dishwasher repairman" might be at the top of your list on the personal side, along with "finish a proposal for a new client" and "make three sales calls" on the business side. Notice how simple each of these items are. While they might seem small, each of them keeps your home running and cash flowing into your business.

Then, I would add items from your time-management checklist. Perhaps you commit to walking for an hour three days a week. Perhaps you need to spend an hour planning your marketing goals for the week or month ahead.

I don't put appointments or family activities on my Big Six list. I put action items—tasks that I must accomplish regardless of time spent with clients, colleagues, carpool, etc.—on my to-do list.

Finally, what are your biggest goals for the year? What can you add that will move you forward? Again, this can be personal or professional.

The point of the Big Six is to focus on what will create momentum and keep you on task and on track. When we create an overwhelmingly long to-do list, we often don't know where to start, or we spend time focusing on activities that don't help us move forward in our business. Remember our time-eating gremlins? To-do lists are another form of those.

I encourage you to create your Big Six a week at a time, knowing things might change and will need to get moved around. Flexibility is essential to a balanced life. One of the aspects of being an entrepreneur that I love most is my ability to course correct midstride. I have goals, I know what I want and need to accomplish, but I am also flexible enough to be able to make quick changes.

Here's what a sample couple days might look like for me.

Monday:
- one-hour walk
- put dinner in slow cooker
- write copy for newsletter
- write sales copy for webinar
- follow up with three past clients
- spend thirty minutes on Facebook

Tuesday:
- one-hour walk
- grocery shopping
- spend thirty minutes on LinkedIn
- work on new opt-in gift for homepage
- research opportunities for speaking engagements
- finish presentation for Thursday morning

Wednesday:
- one-hour walk
- pay property taxes
- final prep for webinar
- print handouts for Thursday morning
- apply to speak to at least three conferences

What do you notice, other than I didn't list any appointments? There is a variety of both personal and professional activities on my Big Six. Putting dinner in the slow cooker may not feel big, but it may ease an overly full day and allow me to have a relaxed dinner with my family. Family dinners are very high on our list of priorities!

Your Instant Insights...

- Tear up your to-do list.
- Prioritize tasks according to deadlines and goals.
- Put no more than six tasks on your daily list that you commit to finishing before going to bed.

Next Step: Add Your Big Six to Your Calendar

The other reason that to-do lists don't work is that they are not connected to your calendar. For creative entrepreneurs, it may feel like a stretch to do this much organization or planning. I promise that if you make planning a habit, it will create the change you want to see in your business and in your life.

The first step in using a calendar effectively is to find the type of calendar that works best for you: digital or paper? I tried using both digital and paper, but that didn't work. I found that I was keeping up with all my appointments on Google calendar and not getting to my Big Six. I was writing them on a paper calendar but didn't always remember to check what I had written down. I would fill my calendar up with appointments, phone calls, and kids' activities, failing to schedule time to get the work done that would move me forward in my business—like marketing myself!

Block out your marketing time on your calendar first! That way you won't fill your day with other activities and leave yourself with little time or energy to complete your marketing tactics. There is no right or wrong system; just pick one and stick with it.

If you choose to work with a paper calendar, make sure you have a day-to-day calendar with plenty of space for writing. It should also include month-at-a-glance pages so you can see upcoming events or programs.

For either a digital or a paper calendar, use color to organize your Big Six. I had one friend who put green around any time that was spent making money. She was a coach, so all her client meetings were green, along with her sales calls. As entrepreneurs, we have lots of hours in the day that don't generate immediate income. We don't get paid by the hour, and we don't get paid to plan, organize, or market ourselves. Make sure there is enough time in your calendar for your money-making activities.

Adding color as an organizing tool is a great way to make writing in your calendar more fun. You can also track the trends of how you are spending your time. I had one member of my sales team whose calendar was inspirational! She had every day organized by the hour and everything color-coded according to the type of task: work, home, kids, sales, etc. At a glance, she knew what was coming.

Too much work and not enough play make Jane a dull girl. Too much play and not enough work make Jane a poor girl. As I said before, this is a juggling act—keep your eye on the ball. Use your calendar as a guiding light, not as a rigid structure. Notice at the end of each week how much you were able to accomplish. I'm still a fan of using gold stars, checking off tasks when they are complete, or other forms of celebrating ourselves. We always have so much to do that we rarely take a moment to celebrate how much we do get done. Often we are doing so much more than we think we are; checking items off the list reminds us of how far we have come.

As you work more with this process, you will discover that your brain dumps don't take as long. You will be able to quickly sort through the list and set priorities. Your Big Six will be obvious each day. You will feel a sense of satisfaction and success. You will feel less overwhelmed and more content with your progress.

Here's a silly example: I was working on the draft of this book and realized I had only about an hour before my next coaching client showed up at my front door. I had taken a one-hour walk with my husband in the morning and hadn't showered or brushed my teeth. I went upstairs to shower and realized that the bathroom counter needed a good cleaning. I had been so focused on writing that I had definitely let some of my housekeeping duties slip. I quickly took everything off the counter, found some cleaner from under the sink, and sprayed the countertop, sinks, and faucets while the shower warmed up. I jumped in the shower, and when I got out, I finished the cleaning. Cleaning the bathroom wasn't on my to-do list, but it needed to get done. I felt such a sense of accomplishment and relief—nothing is worse to me than a dirty bathroom. I went back to writing and working with my client, feeling refreshed and clean on several levels.

I share this to show you that you will get more things done by not overflowing your Big Six to a big sixty. I didn't wait until the last ten minutes to shower. I allowed myself the freedom and flexibility to take five extra minutes to do an unexpected task because I wasn't rushing. Allow the flow of the day to carry you while still committing to your Big Six.

Your Instant Insights...

- Put your Big Six on your calendar.
- Create space in your calendar for interruptions.
- Celebrate your accomplishments.

Make Your Planning Visual – Mind Maps

While there are dozens of apps, websites, and planners on the market that can help you get organized (trust me, I have tried them all!), I have discovered that for my right-brained creative mind I need a visual system. I am a big fan of using mind maps to organize and collect all the information I need.

Mind maps are colorful, playful, and insightful. They help us to visually brainstorm, connect ideas, and embrace our creativity. Anything we can do to make planning more fun is worth a try, right?

Here is a simple definition of a mind map from Wikipedia:

"A **mind map** is a diagram used to visually organize information. A **mind map** is often created around a single concept, drawn as an image in the center of a blank page, to which associated representations of ideas such as images, words and parts of words are added."

For me this means starting with a big sheet of paper, markers, and sticky notes to brainstorm what I need to accomplish. This is similar to our brain dump but more intentional and focused on marketing, content creation, and other business planning that needs to happen. If you are not familiar with mind mapping, watch the video I created for you on how to use a mind map to create blog content:

www.pathtoprofitacademy.com/time-management-book.

For you technology lovers, there is an app for your smart phone and a program for your desktop called SimpleMind that enables you to create mind maps in a digital format. I like how colorful and easy to use this program is, but I know there are other options out there.

I often start by taking a bird's-eye view of the next thirty days in my life and business. I look at what events I have planned, what family activities are on the calendar, and what my marketing goals are. I pay attention to how much time I have open in my calendar between coaching clients, travel, and speaking. Once I have everything in one place, I can start to prioritize and break projects down into manageable, prioritized tasks.

I use this type of planning to organize my blog content, newsletter content, and other ongoing marketing that I need to do on a monthly business.

If you start by just making a giant to-do list, you will create massive pressure on yourself, plus your tasks won't be organized or prioritized in a way that makes sense. By creating a mind map, I can see what I need to accomplish. This is different from a brain dump. A brain dump gets information out of your head and onto paper. A mind map enables you to connect your ideas together and to prioritize them.

Your Instant Insights...

- Use mind maps to create marketing content or brainstorm ideas for your business.

- Adding color and creativity to your planning inspires new ideas.

- Mind maps help you see all the steps needed to complete a particular project or reach a goal.

Time Blocking Will Become Your Best Friend

Time blocking is one of the best time-management tips I have implemented in my business. When I don't do this, I can see where it impacts not only my work-life balance but also my bottom line. I'm just like you—if I don't plan for and commit to my marketing activities, they don't get done on a regular basis. What happens when I'm not marketing? No new clients are flowing in!

Time blocking your calendar means putting your Big Six into specific blocks of time dedicated to the different activities you are committed to accomplishing. You can download an illustration of a calendar using time blocking here:

www.pathtoprofitacademy.com/time-management-book.

The basic concept is to write yourself into your own calendar and to block off time for completing tasks, which could include exercise, putting a pot roast in the slow cooker, making sales calls, or writing a blog post. The secret to success is to take back your time and make your Big Six the highest priority. Who knows? You might get all six done before lunchtime.

Here's a sample of what a day might look like using time blocks:

8:00 a.m. – Exercise

9:00 a.m. to 11:00 a.m. – Marketing

11:00 a.m. – Check e-mail, clear paper clutter

11:30 a.m. – Lunch

12:00 p.m. to 3:00 p.m. – Client calls

3:00 p.m. – Carpool

3:30 p.m. – Social media check-in

4:00 p.m. to 5:00 p.m. – Prepare for next day's presentation

5:00 p.m. – Check e-mail, create Big Six for next day

My husband and I host three-day live workshops called The Path to Profit: Design Your Road Map to Success. In the two weeks coming up to our first event last year, I looked at my calendar and realized that I had filled my calendar with people and not with tasks. I needed time to finalize the content, get files to the printer, and practice the presentation more than I needed to have coffee with a friend. Getting my hair cut was a priority, attending a networking meeting was not. Not claiming space in my calendar caused me to feel stressed out and concerned that I would have sleepless nights leading up to the event. I love to sleep and don't function well when I don't get enough. This was not a good plan! When I realized what I had done, I was able to reschedule people to other times and take back my time.

I can hear many of you creative people asking, "But what about going with the flow? Being flexible?" I often hear my intuitive, creative clients grumbling about structure. You need to make it okay to make changes in your calendar and shift tasks around. You might create a one-hour block that says "marketing," as in the sample above. You commit to spend that one hour doing one of the marketing activities on your list, but you don't need to determine ahead of time exactly which one, especially if there are no deadlines attached.

If you are clear about what needs to get done by when, you can allow more flow into your activities. But you have to start by staking a claim for your creative time, marketing time, and self-care time. Time blocking stops you from overfilling your calendar with people and tasks that don't move you toward your goals.

I have two ways of using time blocking that are visual and colorful. One is using paper and sticky notes, and the other is digital.

I love my Google calendar! I use it for all my appointments and family activities. My husband and I can see each other's calendars, so we know who is where and when. I have also started using my Google calendar for time blocking.

My clients and prospects have access to my online scheduler and can pick times that work for them. If I am not careful and intentional to block out my own work time, I can find myself back in that space of "Oh, crap, when am I going to get this done?" I love looking at my Google calendar and seeing big blocks of time for creative work! Most calendars allow you to color code activities. If you use a digital calendar, make it colorful so that you can see at a glance what you scheduled.

Even though we use a digital calendar, my husband and I are both very visual, so we also have a laminated wall calendar with all our big events, travel dates, and kids' activities on it so that we can easily look ahead to see what's coming up.

I also realized that I felt too trapped and that I didn't have enough detail for my marketing activities using the digital calendar. I love it for managing time and appointments but not activities. I like to use a month-at-a-glance desk-sized paper calendar and sticky notes to organize my content.

You could also use a large white board to do this (or even a poster board) and draw squares on it in bright colors. You can see a visual example of my system here:

www.pathtoprofitacademy.com/time-management-book.

I buy the calendars that don't have dates on them so that I can reuse them. My intention is to be able to see the month's activities at a glance. I use sticky notes for a couple reasons. I love the bright colors! I can break down projects into tiny bites, putting just one step on each sticky note. And finally, I can move the notes around. Freedom and flow stem from this. If I know I have a speech to write and a newsletter to create, I can decide which one I want to work on creating. Or if I have sales calls to make on Monday and they don't get done, I move the sticky note to Tuesday.

Once a task is complete, I get to toss the sticky note and do a happy dance, which feels oh, so good! By the end of the week, there should be no sticky notes left. And if there are, you can go back to the list of questions from chapter 8 and decide if and when you will get that particular task done.

Your Instant Insights...

- Create space in your calendar for what matters most. Block out the time needed to get tasks done.

- Allow for creative flow inside the time blocks you create.

- Use a wall-sized calendar and sticky notes to keep it visual and flexible.

Change Your Business or Go Out of Business: How Committed Are You?

A couple of years ago I was surfing through a free e-book I had in my download folder. It was just one of many e-books full of marketing ideas, tips on attracting clients, blogging ideas, and secrets to business success that I had downloaded when launching my coaching practice. I love free stuff, and I was easily attracted to the bright, shiny promise of the next new marketing tactic that would lead to my overnight success, even though I know what I needed to be doing most days to build my business.

The truth is that it's easier to download a free e-book or buy a $14.99 product that we hope will change our life than it is to actually knuckle down and do the work required to be successful.

Getting into action changed my personal life and created my business success!

As I was rapidly scanning the PDF file on my computer, this statement caught my eye: "Change Your Business or Go Out of Business." *Wow*, I thought, *that's so true*. The author, E.G. Sebastian, went on to say, "Every day I meet so many business owners who simply refuse to do things differently, but yet, they expect different results. That's the textbook definition of insanity. You must be willing to change your advertising, marketing, production, and any and everything else, in order to survive during this new economy. That's the truth, plain and simple." *Uh huh*, I thought, *yep, that's the conversation I have been having with my clients over the past few months. But wait ... uh oh ... does this ring true for me, too? Well, of course it does!*

When I had that aha moment that I was treating my business like a hobby, I knew it was time to make some changes. I kept saying I wanted to be successful and to make money, but I wasn't following my words with the right actions.

Below I share the three strategies that I have implemented in the past two years that took me from a part-time business coach to a six-figure coach with a thriving business model.

Strategy #1 – Commitment

At the top of the list is COMMITMENT to my own success, which means doing whatever it takes to get the number of clients I need to reach my financial goals. Commitment is a mindset. I invite you to investigate whether your actions are in alignment with your stated goals.

Strategy #2 – Become a Time Tyrant

Being a Time Tyrant means creating an organized, strategic calendar based on my goals; sticking to the tasks that I set for myself; and managing my time-eating gremlins.

Strategy #3 – Clarity Matters More than Anything

In order to be an effective Time Tyrant without feeling totally overwhelmed and exhausted, you need crystal clarity about your financial and life goals. Most of my clients think they need expensive and expansive marketing plans that take lots of time and money. The truth is that if you can answer the following five questions, you can create your entire time block around your answers.

1) Do I know exactly who my client is and what her problems are?

2) Do I know why I am the best person to solve her problems?

3) Do I know how many clients I need to make my financial goals?

4) Do I know how many people I need to contact to get that many clients?

5) Do I know what the best marketing activities are to get me in front of my prospective clients?

This may sound complex or challenging, but I guarantee that if you figure this piece out and you commit 100 percent to doing what it takes, success will come. It will not come overnight, but it will come. Once you have your strategy in place and you implement the time-management and brainstorming activities we discussed in this book, you will have the exact strategy you need to build your profitable business without sacrificing your time or your lifestyle.

Your Instant Insights...

- Business success requires commitment followed by action.
- Increase your productivity by becoming a Time Tyrant.
- Get crystal clear about your goals and action steps.

About the Author

Who is Minette Riordan, Ph.D.

- Are you tired of constantly being stressed out about time and money?

- Are you being pressured by family or . friends to get your business going or to give it up?

- Do you feel like you have tried everything to build a profitable business and nothing has worked?

Believe me, I get it. I have been exactly where you are. I have answered yes to each of those questions. I have been overwhelmed, overworked, disconnected from my self and my family, broke, depressed and just plain mad that I couldn't figure out how to make publishing company profitable.

It all starts with creating the right business model that supports all of the roles you play as a woman business owner: entrepreneur, visionary, leader, mother, wife, lover, daughter, sister and friend. Yes, you can create a thriving, profitable business and still have a personal life, too. I know it can be done, because that's my life now.

In summer of 2012, my husband and I made a dramatic change to our lives – we uprooted ourselves and our two kids after 13 years in the

Dallas, TX area and relocated to sunny Santa Barbara, CA. I sold my business and started over – new friends, new business, and only a vague idea of what I wanted to do next.

Moving our family from Texas to California was hard. I can still remember my kids crying on that last day of school as we prepared to leave the only home they had ever known. I remember standing in my empty house and thinking, it's not our home anymore... but all the challenges, tears and changes were worth it.

It was a challenge to start over. My identity as the owner of Scissortail Publishing was crystal clear for over a decade, I knew who I was and what I needed to do every single day to grow my business. I had a staff to support me and great mentors and advisors.

Suddenly, I didn't have the words to describe what I was doing or how I wanted to help others. I didn't have a team to bounce ideas off of and I realized I wasn't even sure where to start building my coaching practice. I went from being the owner of a 6-figure multi-media publishing company to being a coach, but what kind of coach? Who did I want to coach?

One day my husband said to me, "I don't know what to tell people you do..." Yikes, it was time for some clarity and certainty. What I learned in my own journey is that clarity is the foundation stone for business success. Without clarity, we tend to flop around like fish out of water. So I did the work to get clear, I hired a coach and created a business model that I loved. I became crystal clear that I love working with creative women. The more clear that I became, the more the clients showed up.

In 2016, my husband was able to quit his full time job of 20 years to come work full time with me in our thriving coaching and training business. Our kids are 17 and 14, being present in their lives is so important right now and we are here when they get home from school. I love that they walk into our office every afternoon after school and share how their day went and ask how we are. That flexibility and availability have always been super important to us; in fact many of our business and lifestyle decisions were made because of our core values around family, commitment and connection.

Plus, my husband and I get to spend more time together than we have in the last 20 years of married life. Working full time and raising children is hard work. There were many times when we realized that between work and kids, we weren't making enough time to continue to grow as a couple. Now it's not unusual to find us walking on the beach in the middle of our workday. We lead a much different lifestyle than we did before – a lifestyle that we worked hard to create.

Living with this kind of purpose is so exciting and I thrilled with our new adventure. Building a coaching practice has been an incredible gift in my life. I have the privilege of spending my days helping creative women entrepreneurs turn their big dreams into big profits.

Books

From Fizzle to Sizzle: Four Crucial Tools for Relationship Repair

The Artful Marketer: The Fundamental Business Guide for Creative Entrepreneurs

Education

Prior to starting her publishing company, Minette was an educator who earned her Ph.D. from Stanford University in 1995. She has a BA from Texas A&M University and an MA from the University of Texas at Austin. She has taught at the university and high school levels, as well as adult education and personal development workshops.

Certifications

Minette is a lifelong learner and holds a variety of certifications from the following organizations. She hasn't stopped studying since she completed her PhD in 1995. She uses all of these different tools to help her clients to build a profitable business that is meaningful, creative and fun!

- 2006 - Certified Coach for Parents - Academy for Parent Coaching International
- 2007 - CRG Licensed Facilitator – Personal Style Indicator
- 2013 - Life Optimization Coach – Life Optimization Coaching
- 2012 - SoulCollage® facilitator
- 2014 - Sacred Money Archetypes Coach
- 2014 - Zentangle® teacher
- 2015 - ARTbundance coach
- 2015 – Money Breakthrough Method Coach
- 2016 – Creatively Fit Coach

Awards

Dr. Riordan received the 2007 Altrusa Outstanding Women of Today award and was named the 2009 Small Business Owner of the Year by the Plano Chamber of Commerce. In 2011, the Texas Home Child Care Association honored her with the Libby Linebarger award for her commitment to education.

Media

Dr. Minette Riordan has been featured in numerous television and radio interviews on ABC, CBS, TimeWarner and Fox Radio. She also hosted her own radio show on talk radio in the

Dallas area and been featured on over 100 radio and podcast interviews nationwide.

Learn more about Minette and her work at:

www.minetteriordan.com
www.pathtoprofitacademy.com

Connect with the Author

Websites: www.MinetteRiordan.com
www.PathtoProfitAcademy.com

E-mail: Minette@minetteriordan.com

Social Media:

Facebook:
http://www.facebook.com/pathtoprofitacademy

LinkedIn:
http://www.linkedin.com/in/minetteriordan

Other Books by this Author

The Artful Marketer:
The Fundamental Business Guide for Creative Entrepreneurs

From Fizzle to Sizzle:
Four Crucial Tools for Relationship Repair

About Crescendo Publishing

Crescendo Publishing is a boutique-style, concierge VIP publishing company assisting entrepreneurs with writing, publishing, and promoting their books for the purposes of lead-generation and achieving global platform growth, then monetizing it for even more income opportunities.

Check out some of our latest best-selling AuthorPreneurs at http://crescendopublishing.com/new-authors/.

About the Instant Insights™ Book Series

The *Instant Insights™ Book Series* is a fact-only, short-read, book series written by EXPERTS in very specialized categories. These high-value, high-quality books can be produced in ONLY 6-8 weeks, from concept to launch, in BOTH PRINT & eBOOK Formats!

This book series is FOR YOU if:

- You are an expert in your niche or area of specialty
- You want to write a book to position yourself as an expert
- You want YOUR OWN book – NOT a chapter in someone else's book
- You want to have a book to give to people when you're speaking at events or simply networking
- You want to have it available quickly
- You don't have the time to invest in writing a 200-page full book
- You don't have a ton of money to invest in the production of a full book – editing, cover design, interior layout, best-seller promotion

- You don't have a ton of time to invest in finding quality contractors for the production of your book – editing, cover design, interior layout, best-seller promotion

For more information on how you can become an *Instant Insights™* author, visit **www.InstantInsightsBooks.com**

More Books in the
Instant Insight™ Series

A Time Management System *for* Creative Entrepreneurs	Branding and Website Essentials *for* Entrepreneurs	How to Create & Build a Successful Beauty Business	Organizing Your Workspace for a Productivity Boost
How to Be a Happy *&* Prosperous CEO	Taking Your Business from Startup to Thrive in 45 Days	7 Strategies *for* Raising Calm, Inspired, & Successful Children	Creating a Solid, Lasting Connection with Your Kids
12 Leadership Powers *for* Successful Women	MOTIVATION! Your Master Key to Success & Riches	PERFORMANCE POWER: Clarity, Confidence & Joy	Practical Natural Healing Tips for Vibrant Living

Crescendo
CrescendoPublishing.com

Made in the USA
Lexington, KY
22 June 2016